TASTING BIRTH
AND DEATH

An Introduction to the Meditation System called 'The Four
Thoughts that Turn the Mind to Dharma'

JAMPA THAYE

Contents

Introduction

The practice of dharma, the teachings of the Buddha, strips away the delusions that obscure the true nature of our mind and keep us locked in suffering. Meditation is the essence of the Buddha's teachings and this booklet gives some guidance on the system of meditation known as 'The Four Thoughts that Turn the Mind to Dharma.' These meditations especially bring about the quality of renunciation. Renunciation means letting go of attachment to worldly things and is the essential foundation of all dharma practices.

The concept of renunciation is very important in dharma since it is easy for us to mistake the meaning of this term. We may think of it merely as external renunciation, such as the taking of monastic vows. Whilst such vows may be very beneficial if we have the right aptitudes and circumstances in our life, we must not confuse the adoption of external patterns of behaviour with real renunciation. Dharma is essentially a process of stripping away all that is obscuring our potential for enlightenment, our buddha nature. Therefore adoption of any special kind of lifestyle or characteristics may, in some cases, actually create a further level of obscuration.

What is true renunciation? It is the simplification of our life and attitudes. As the great Atisha says, 'Always shed complexity, always simplify your life in order to keep your dharma practice alive'. Therefore renunciation is actually about letting go. Before we seriously engage with the dharma teachings, we have many pursuits, many ambitions and many objects with which we surround ourselves, all of which we feel to be absolutely necessary to our security and happiness. In fact, not only are these things unnecessary for happiness, they are actually entanglements which further alienate us from buddha nature. We have to let go of these things.

This letting go should be understood in a very joyful way. If one realises that one has been unnecessarily tying oneself up in knots over something that is completely useless, one's feeling when released is one of delight and pleasure. So it should not be understood as something grim or artificial, or the imposition of some very hard task upon us, but as something extremely pleasing, light and spacious. This is the simplicity of renunciation.

The Four Thoughts

THE MANY DHARMA teachings may be categorised into three 'vehicles' or 'yanas': the hinayana (lesser vehicle), mahayana (great vehicle) and vajrayana (indestructible vehicle). The Four Thoughts are the fundamental teachings of the first of these, the hinayana, and as such are the foundation of the entire dharma. Ultimately they come from the discourses (sutras) of Lord Buddha, but the particular form explained here derives from the teachings of such masters as Nagarjuna and Shantideva. These were great Buddhist masters who lived after the passing of Lord Buddha and gave many teachings that made the dharma easier to understand and practise.

The true nature of our mind is buddha nature, which bears the qualities of wisdom, compassion and power. But right now we cannot really experience those qualities because the 'three poisons' of desire, hatred and ignorance obscure them. The very first thing we must do is begin to disentangle ourselves from the veils caused by these three poisons. This process begins by using the fundamental teachings of the Four Thoughts.

Unlike the very subtle teachings of the vajrayana and mahayana, the Four Thoughts are very earthy and uncomplicated. They connect immediately with the ordinary facts of our experience, which is exactly where we observe the effects of desire, aggression and delusion. Through these four reflections one comes to taste the undiluted reality of birth and death. In that sense, these teachings are very uncompromising. If we follow them properly and develop a sense of them in our heart, it is as if we have come into contact with the blood and guts of our own life. There is no attempt in these teachings to make pretty the work of the three poisons, since they create nothing but unhappiness for us. Nor is there any attempt to mystify by indulgence in elaborate metaphysics or philosophy.

When we begin to see the nature of birth and death, the basic parameters of our life, an unfeigned and genuine renunciation will arise. It is like we are in a burning house and we will immediately want to rush out. When we have heard and reflected upon these teachings, we will want only liberation.

How are these teachings to be used? They are instructions to be meditated upon. Often in the West it is understood that meditation is merely an exercise in sitting quietly and abandoning conceptualisation. Settling meditation (Tib: 'jog-bsgom) is very good as a preliminary, but there must also be analytical meditation (Tib: *spyad-bsgom*). All full meditation systems use both these types of practice. The Four Thoughts are to be used as a form of the latter, analytical or reflective meditation. They are not merely doctrinal lists that we can listen to, read once or twice, and say that we either agree or disagree with them. That would miss the point. They are designed to open pathways within our life, allowing us to see the structure of our world clearly. The particular ways they are presented in the texts are simply pointers. We transform them into effective methods by reflecting over their meaning. It is important to understand from the beginning that what is written in the texts is not an exhaustive description but a set of hints and questions to use and work with. This booklet serves as a guide for such reflection. One must go back to it again and again.

Of course, the presence of a master who can instruct us fully in these meditation systems is absolutely necessary here, as with all of Buddha's teachings. Therefore any Buddhist manual or book such as this must be used in conjunction with the oral teachings of one's masters if it is to be effective.

Precious Human Birth

LORD BUDDHA TAUGHT that all sentient beings possess the potential to achieve liberation, and he called this potential 'buddha nature'. However, as with any seed, the environment in which it is located is essential for its fruition. If one considers an ordinary seed, one may see that it has within itself the full potential to manifest as a particular kind of fruit or flower but it needs appropriate conditions such as good soil, rain etc. in which to grow. What is the correct environment for the fruition of buddha nature? The great patriarch of the Kagyu tradition of Buddhism, Gampopa, says in the *Jewel Ornament of Liberation* that whilst buddha nature is the cause of enlightenment, its support is a precious human birth. In other words, only those who have obtained a particular kind of human birth are in a position to bring the potential for enlightenment to fruition.

This recognition is the starting point of dharma. Buddhist practice does not begin with some complex metaphysical theory, remote from everyday experience, or some kind of tantric practice. It begins right here in the present moment. Where are we now? What is here? We have the fact of being human in this particular situation and the fact that it is such a wonderful opportunity. Just as in settling meditation, where the main focus is mindfulness of the present moment, so it is with the Four Thoughts. They bring one back to the reality of the present moment.

The veils of our ignorance are so strong that we have never really woken up to the fact of what it means to be human. We take our human status for granted. It is of little significance to us and we waste it. If we wake up to its importance, we will use this opportunity skilfully and wisely in order to accomplish buddhahood. How then do we wake up to its importance? We reflect on its preciousness.

Human birth is precious for two reasons. Firstly, it has conditions that other forms of life lack which are necessary for the qualities of enlightenment to come to fruition, such as the capacity to understand and practise the teachings. Secondly, it is extremely rare to be born as a human. It is not inevitable in this universe that we have a human life. The universe is not ordered so that we will be born human. In fact human life is very rare because the universe is endless.

One might object that somewhere in other world systems there may be beings who are not human but are quite capable of practising dharma. However, the teaching on precious human birth does not mean that it is only our species that can practise dharma. If there were beings who had different organic structures and who looked completely different to us, but had all the same attributes of consciousness, then although we might not normally consider them 'human', we could call them such from a dharma point of view. So humanity in a dharma sense refers to a particular kind of consciousness rather than the physical characteristics of a particular species. After all, why should enlightenment only be possible on earth? Enlightenment is nothing more than waking up to what is real and so can be present anywhere in this endless universe.

There are four points of view from which one can understand the rarity of human birth; cause, number, example and nature. These form the principal reflections for meditation on precious human birth.

1. Cause

Everything in the universe arises from a combination of causes and conditions. We can meditate on the rarity of precious human birth therefore by reflecting on the rarity of its causes. The most important quality of true humanity is virtue. Since effects always resemble their causes, one can understand that the principal cause of precious human birth is virtuous behaviour. If we behave self-indulgently and abusively now, i.e. non-virtuously, then we alienate ourselves from our humanity and create a pattern for the future loss of human life. If we look around us now, we will see that actions done out of regard for others are rare. Since the causes are rare then the result, human birth, will also be rare. Reflecting on this situation is how one meditates on precious human birth from the point of view of *cause*.

2. Number

When we consider the number of humans compared to the total number of living beings, we can see that humanity is very rare. Indeed, in comparison with other forms of sentient life in this infinite universe it is numerically infinitesimal. If we lift up a single stone in the summertime, we will see a countless number of insects, far more than in an entire town of human beings. Therefore the total number of sentient lives is vast in comparison with the number that possess human characteristics.

Furthermore, it is not just the physical possession of a human body that is described as precious, but its endowment with freedom, intelligence and contact with the dharma. The number of humans endowed with these characteristics is even less. Reflecting in this way, one can easily understand the rarity of precious human birth from the point of view of *number*.

3. Example

This meditation is explained in Shantideva's great work, *Entering the Bodhisattva Conduct,*

> It is because of this the Buddha
>   said
> That the difficulty of attaining a
>   human birth
> Is like a turtle putting its neck
>   through
> A wooden yoke adrift on a great
>   ocean.

This is a very famous analogy, first presented by Lord Buddha in the sutras and then later by Nagarjuna and Shantideva. Imagine that there is a blind turtle who is swimming in the ocean and can only rise to the surface once every one hundred years. Moreover, there are winds that are tossing a wooden yoke about from one side of the ocean to the other. The turtle's task is to put its neck through the yoke that is floating on top of the ocean. It is said that once human birth has been lost, to attain it again is even more difficult than that.

One might think this sounds unrealistically hard, that human birth cannot possibly be so rare. But why should it not be so rare? There is no god ordering the universe, so there is nobody responsible for our own situation but us. Our present situation has come about through our actions. If we act in such a way as to negate our humanity then we will experience its loss in future lives. The opportunity to regain it is very rare. How can one develop those humane characteristics again if one is not in that state?

4. Nature

The reason why the human birth acts as the uniquely suitable basis for the attainment of buddhahood is that it embodies freedom and good conditions. This is what is meant by contemplating the rarity of human birth by its 'nature'. The way we meditate on these is to consider its freedom in terms of the *eight freedoms* and its good conditions in terms of the *ten positive conditions*. One might ask if these are definitive lists. They are not definitive but merely guides or pointers for us to work with. If we see other things that make us appreciate our freedom and opportunity then we can incorporate those into our understanding as well. Contemplating in this way awakens one to the wondrous opportunity one now has to achieve liberation and cuts through the tendency to drift through life, taking it for granted.

The Eight Freedoms

These describe our freedom from eight kinds of negative situation. The first four negative situations are rebirth as a:

1. Hell being
2. Ghost
3. Animal
4. God

These are situations in which the possibility of practising dharma is absent. In the realm of hell beings or ghosts, our minds are so clouded by the projections of hatred and avarice respectively, that there is no opportunity to turn to dharma. Similarly, if reborn as an animal, possessing their shrunken horizons, there is no way to even distinguish good and evil, let alone practise dharma. If we are born as a god, we will be so intoxicated by temporary pleasures that again there will not be any space for self-examination and reflection, which are necessary for dharma.

One might ask, is it really possible for me to be reborn in such states? As we will see in the section on 'the defects of samsara', whilst such states are not ultimately real or permanent, they are nonetheless realistic experiences which are made by mind. One should consider the fact that the humanity I now possess is not something intrinsic or godgiven, but simply a result of my previous virtuous actions. Similarly, these non-human states are possible for me because they arise simply through my own actions.

There are also four negative situations that are found in human life, which prevent it from being a *precious* human life. This means that although one has a human body, it is not possible to practise dharma. These are rebirth as:

1. A fool
2. A barbarian
3. Possessing wrong views

4. Living at a time when no buddha has
    appeared

To be born a *fool* (Tib: *lkugs pa*) can be understood in
modern terms as being born as somebody who,
although possessing human consciousness, has a brain
so damaged that their consciousness cannot fully work
in this life. Such a person cannot engage in the dharma,
because they are imprisoned by the defects of their
existence.

A *barbarian* means somebody who is born into a
human environment in which there are not even the
rudiments of moral culture, without which there can be
no humane behaviour.

Possessing wrong views primarily means a complete
refusal to open up to the connection between actions
and results. For example, refusing to acknowledge that
suffering is caused by negative actions. This refusal is
not something that one is actually born with, but if one
develops such a severe inflexibility of mind that one
cannot develop moral behaviour, and one will be
blocked from practising dharma.

Living at a time when no buddha has appeared means to
be born into a period of history when there are no
teachings of any buddha still in existence.

If we look at our own situation by running through
these eight factors, we can see that we are free from
them and should feel energised and positive. Concen-
trating on precious human birth gives us strength and
confidence. Because in dharma we talk about suffering,

people sometimes think that dharma is very negative and oppressive. In this presentation we begin with precious human birth in order to endow ourselves with the necessary feelings of strength and encouragement. Look upon that as the first step in dharma, because if one does not have a feeling of joy then one will not be able to persist with the dharma.

The Ten Positive Conditions

Even if one has the eight freedoms, in order to be able to practise dharma many conditions must be met in one's life. These are described by the *ten positive conditions*. Of these, there are five that occur directly in us and five that occur through others. The five that occur directly in our own life are:

1. Being born as a human being
2. Living in a land where dharma is practised
3. Possessing sound senses
4. Possessing faith in dharma
5. Having refrained from committing any of the 'five heinous actions'

If we had been born an animal, or did not live in a land where dharma is practised, even if we were free from other negative conditions, then how could our potential for enlightenment be fulfilled? If there is no way of watering a seed, it will never grow into a flower. In the same way, we need the dharma in our lives if our potential for buddhahood is to be fulfilled. We possess sound senses, so we can understand the teachings. We possess faith in the dharma and so wish to practise it. We have not committed the actions of great gravity such as killing one's parents. These are actions that produce such a profound alienation in us that the spaciousness needed for dharma practice will not occur in this life.

There are also five conditions that occur external to us:

1. A buddha has appeared
2. The buddha has taught the dharma
3. The teachings still exist
4. There are genuine followers of the teachings
5. There are those who have compassion and support one's practice

Since a buddha has appeared one might assume that such an occurrence is common. But why should it be? So much of human culture is a diversion from the possibility of awakening that it is actually not a likelihood at all that somebody in history should have awakened. Nor is it likely that such a person should have taught the doctrine. Nor are any of the other conditions likely, since there are so many factors working against them. For all these conditions to have been met in our lifetime is an extremely rare and fortuitous occurrence.

The eighteen conditions are not to be thought of as meaningless lists but as reflections that bring home how human life has arisen out of many causes and conditions, making it infinitely precious. If just one of the positive conditions were absent, or one of the negative conditions present, then even if we possessed all the other seventeen, there would be no possibility for us to practise dharma in this lifetime.

Meditation on Precious Human Birth

We work with this teaching by reflecting on the four ways in which human birth is precious. For example, one recalls the ten positive conditions and spends some time thinking about each one, how it applies to me and how it is not to be taken for granted. We need therefore to memorise them, not because they are a set of rules or doctrines but simply so that we can work with them.

In that way we develop a sense of the rarity of human birth. Having obtained such a precious human birth as rare as this, what an act of folly it would be to squander it, what stupidity to get such a wonderful opportunity and then waste it. That is why Nagarjuna, the second buddha, says in his *Letter to a Friend*,

> One who, having obtained a
>   human birth, commits non
>   virtue,
> Is far more foolish even than one
> Who cleans up vomit
> Using a jewel-adorned golden
>   vessel.

Elsewhere it says that being born human is like being a jewel merchant who suddenly finds himself on an island where all the ordinary stones are actually jewels. If he returned empty-handed from that island he would be unbelievably stupid. Similarly, if at the end of this life we leave without any positive qualities through not practising dharma, we would be as foolish as that merchant.

Impermanence

WHILST PRECIOUS HUMAN birth is about recognising what is here now, one must also understand it will not last forever since everything is transient. Meditation on impermanence overcomes the danger of developing complacency when contemplating precious human birth. Most importantly, impermanence means death. Contemplating death prevents us from understanding impermanence in a merely theoretical way so that our hearts are unable to engage with it. After all, most people would sign up to the idea of impermanence without really understanding what it means. Impermanence means death, not just any old death but our own death, the end of this precious human life. Therefore meditating on impermanence is pre-eminently meditating on death.

The system of meditation presented here has three main topics of contemplation, each of which is divided into three subtopics.

1. Death is Certain

One might think that the certainty of death is obvious. However such thinking is too abstract and theoretical. One has to contemplate the significance of death for 'me', because it seems that although one can intellectually sign up to impermanence one can simultaneously harbour a childish sense that one is protected from death. Some, such as the modern materialist, hope for a death which is completely unconscious and which will remain so forevermore. This is another attempt to flee from the reality of death. However, death cannot be avoided and we will definitely experience it.

There are three subtopics to meditate on in order to realise the certainty of death.

1A. Nobody has avoided death

This is a very simple point but one of devastating consequence for one's preconceptions. Nobody in history has avoided death, so how can I avoid it? It is certain to befall me. We could look at the world as being like a graveyard.

We are walking on the deposits of all those who lived before us. As Patrul Rinpoche tells us in *The Words of my Perfect Teacher*,

 No matter whether they were great heroes or great religious beings, the beings of the past have all passed away.

Thus even Lord Buddha showed the reality of impermanence in his death. As Shantideva says in *Entering the Bodhisattva Conduct*,

> If, without respite, day and night,
> This life is running out,
> And there is no granting of an
> extension,
> Why would death not come for
> someone like me?

1B. Life is compound

The inevitability of death is evident in the decay and collapse that are woven into the very fabric of the universe. Impermanence is the law that pervades everything. Life itself, based as it is on the temporary union of body and mind, is part of that fabric. A life is not a solid entity, but is contingent upon the coming together of causes and conditions. Everything produced in this way will eventually fall apart. As Thogme Zangpo says,

> Family and friends of long
> standing will be parted, one
> by one;
> Wealth and property acquired
> through hard work will be left
> behind;
> The guesthouse of the body will be

> abandoned by consciousness,
> its guest.
> To renounce this life is the practice
> of a Conqueror's child.

Our life began with the fusion of sperm and ovum. Therefore, it is compound and must eventually come apart. We should look within ourselves to determine what possible element of our body and mind could be permanent. What I consider to be 'me' is just an aggregation, a compounded phenomenon, not something elemental or intrinsic. There is nothing here whatsoever with the characteristic of permanence.

1C. Everything is moving towards its end

From the very moment of conception life is running out and death is rushing to meet us. With each moment life is becoming shorter. For example, do we understand that this is actually what we are acknowledging when we celebrate our birthdays? The traditional analogy is to consider that life is like an arrow shot into the sky. It may fly far or a very short distance, but eventually it will reach the end of its journey. Or we could consider the analogy of an execution. It is like each one of us is sentenced to death. We do not know when it will be carried out, but the sentence is absolutely certain.

We should consider these certainties until the imaginary bubble of protection that we surround ourselves with is dissolved. Death is certain and it *will* happen to me. That understanding alone should bring complete realism and an enhanced sense of the preciousness of the present moment. We should ask, what have I been doing with my life and what have I been spending it in the pursuit of? It is so precious, so wonderful, yet what is all this junk that I have filled it up with and which I think is so important? In the light of the certainty of death, one can easily let go of any attachment. As Shantideva says,

> Having blocked off all paths,
> The Lord of Death is now looking
>   for you.
> How can you enjoy food?
> How can you enjoy sleep?

2. The Time of Death is Uncertain

One's ego might still be able to dilute the power of this teaching by thinking that death is certain but will occur at some time in the distant future. We can be blinded to the certainty of death in this way. To combat this there is a further series of contemplations on the point that the time of death is uncertain.

2A. One's life span is not fixed

There is no fixed span of life for human beings and no guaranteed tenure. As it is said,

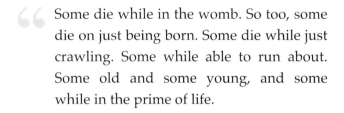

> Some die while in the womb. So too, some die on just being born. Some die while just crawling. Some while able to run about. Some old and some young, and some while in the prime of life.

Which of those will happen to us, we cannot say. We cannot say at all when death will befall us. So how can I think that I can put off dharma practice until later?

2B. There are many causes of death

There is a multiplicity of dangers to life, many things that can upset this fragile, temporary integration of body and mind. There are very many physical causes that can bring about death and even some mental causes. Human life is not secure or protected, but a fragile existence, like a bubble on water. People in good health and comparatively young can be struck down suddenly. Even tiny things can kill us. There is nothing we can do to be secure in this body.

2C. Even the supports of life can become causes of death

To emphasise one's appreciation of the uncertainty of the time of death, one reflects over the point that even the things that usually support life such as food and medical treatment can sometimes be fatal.

So in these three ways the time of death is not certain. Reflecting on these will bring us back to the present moment, because that is all we really have and is the only time we can be sure of our ability to practise dharma.

3. Only Dharma Will Help at the Time of Death

What exactly will help us at the time of death, when our mind and body separate, as they eventually must? At that time, the body will return to the elements but mind will travel on alone to the next life through the intermediate stage. Can we be sure of this? Mind is not a physical compound and has none of the qualities of a material substance. Therefore it cannot be burnt, dissolved, or evaporated into space. Mind or consciousness derives only from its own continuum, so the destruction of the physical form cannot bring about the destruction of the mind. How comforting it would be if there were just a blankness at death, because then there would be a complete absence of suffering and no need to experience the consequences of one's actions. Sadly, such wishful thinking is not true. Mind will continue after death.

What can help us at that time? We could spend our whole lives developing physical strength or gaining allies and possessions, but how will such things help us when we come to die? No amount of physical strength and no army can prevent one being taken by death. As Jetsun Milarepa says,

 Death is already inside us, symbolised by

the skeleton that exists within our physical form.

The accumulation of wealth will not help us, nor the number of books we have read, nor the amount of scholarly knowledge we have accumulated, nor the extent of our cultural refinement. We cannot philosophise death away with eloquent arguments. Why pursue these things as if life depended upon it, when they will not help at all? The bodhisattva of wisdom, Manjushri, said,

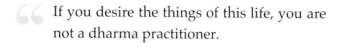 If you desire the things of this life, you are not a dharma practitioner.

We need to look at our life whilst contemplating impermanence and see what is dharma and what is not. That which is not dharma will be of no use at the time of death.

Just as the first two meditations on impermanence had three parts, so it is here. According to Gampopa's *Jewel Ornament of Liberation*, one meditates on the uselessness of wealth, friends and one's own body at the time of death. One can meditate on these or whatever else one has attachment to.

We develop renunciation through realising the uselessness of worldly things, letting them go as being of no interest or importance. It is the imprints of one's virtuous and nonvirtuous actions that go with the mind after death. If I want my mind to be accompanied by positive conditions when I die then I should use my life to practise virtue, caring for others. If I want to achieve liberation at the time of death then I must practise meditation in order to realise the clear light nature of my mind. These two things, virtuous actions and meditation practice, comprise the whole of dharma and only these will help us.

Meditation on Impermanence

One meditates on impermanence by reflecting again and again on each of these points. For example, one considers the analogy of the arrow until one gets a sense of how death is certain to arrive. The more one considers them, the more real the truth of impermanence will become. Thus, the clinging to insignificant objects and ambitions will diminish.

The teaching on impermanence is not morbid or depressing but energising. It compels us to seize the great opportunity that is here now in this precious human life. Rather than gloominess, a sign of developing conviction in impermanence is a feeling of lightness and spaciousness. There is less baggage to cling onto and many worries and concerns simply fade into insignificance. This awareness intensifies the beauty of the present moment, this limitless opportunity in which we can do so much if we only wake up to the fact that we are alive.

Karma, Action and Result

TO FURTHER UNDERSTAND the power and significance of this present moment in our human life, one should think about karma. Karma means actions. The entire range of situations that comprise our lives have their roots in our actions. No external power or random chance has contrived our present position in the cycle of birth and death, but it derives from our own past deeds. We have the potential to create a wholesome future in which we can practise dharma or a destructive, negative future in which we are alienated from dharma. Contemplating this brings about a further maturation of our status as human beings, since we understand the power our situation gives to us.

In other systems of thought, such as theism or materialism, there is always a means of avoiding responsibility for one's situation. In theistic systems, one blames external forces such as God or the devil. Materialists may blame genes, random chance, or politics. We can blame all of these things but actually the responsibility for our situation with its particular strengths and weaknesses lies here in our own actions.

Karma does not mean we are imprisoned in a world where everything arises through blind fate or predestination. Karma actually liberates us because it puts control of our life in our hands. We are free to determine our own future. Thus karma should not be understood in an overly simplistic or naïve way. In fact, it is said that karma is only completely understood by a buddha. Nonetheless, one should have at least some understanding of how karma operates in order to avoid naivety or superstition.

How Karma is Accumulated

Every action one performs, whether physical, verbal or mental, deposits an imprint in the continuum of mind. Since beginningless time, we have been accumulating these imprints through our continual positive, negative and neutral actions and they have been ripening as our positive, negative and neutral experiences respectively.

The primary root that determines the karmic quality of an action is the intention from which the action springs. As it says in Vasubhandu's *Abhidharmakosa*,

> What is karma? Karma is intention and what results from intention.

The actual commission of the action by body or

speech is secondary. It is even the case that an intention without a physical action leaves a karmic imprint, since an intention is a mental action. Mind is the king of all appearances because it precedes all actions of body and speech and determines their qualities. This is very important because instead of merely looking at external activities we should look always to the mind. It is even possible that what may appear to an observer to be a bad action might in reality be a good action if it arises from the right intention and a clear understanding of what is beneficial in the situation.

How Karma Ripens

Virtuous and non-virtuous actions mature as various forms of happiness and suffering respectively. This is the crucial point about karma. We should not approach it by speculating on the particular details of how actions may ripen. Similarly, we cannot use this teaching to make judgements about the experiences of others. Since it is the mind that primarily bears the results of our previous actions, we cannot see or judge the karma of other people because we cannot see into their minds.

For example, one might be tempted to say, "He got knocked over by a bus; that must be a result of his previous evil actions". Such an attitude is completely inappropriate. We should not get involved in simplistic mechanical interpretations of how certain events may be caused. It is said that only a buddha understands karma because only a buddha is totally free from it. Therefore whilst talking about karma and taking it seriously for ourselves means committing ourselves to moral behaviour, we should also be very careful and reticent about judging others.

In the sutras, it is taught that karma ripens in four ways.

1. The active fruit in harmony with the cause

The primary way in which karma works is that it ripens into tendencies to behave in certain ways. This ripening occurs through the stream of mind because karma is primarily mental. Every time we act, or every time there is a conscious volition, an imprint is deposited within our mindstream. Specifically, it is deposited at the level of mind that is called the 'base consciousness', or *alaya vijnana*. That imprint is a tendency to behave in a certain way, which will occur at a future time when the appropriate conditions arise. Just as an ordinary seed may be planted in the earth but may not ripen for six months depending on the conditions of sunlight, rain etc., so it is with these tendencies of our mind. They ripen as a particular result only when the appropriate conditions are there.

For example, someone from an Islamic country is offered the opportunity to indulge in alcohol whilst abroad. He decides to drink it, and thus has his first experience of alcohol. He finds it pleasant. Then he returns home where there is no alcohol and the thought never arises in his mind. Upon returning to the West and finding alcohol available again, it occurs to him to have another drink, because the tendency has already been imprinted in his mindstream. Thus the imprint was created through action, then lay dormant in the mind, then came to fruition as an intention to repeat the action once the right conditions arose.

Another example is the brutality that can develop once the act of killing has occurred. Once someone has killed, the tendency to kill again is imprinted in the mind which makes it easier to do so again. Thus karma works through the imprinting of tendencies in the mind stream.

2. The passive fruit in harmony with the cause

The fruit of deeds can also ripen in experiences that are similar to their causes. An example of this would be the way in which killing can generate a vulnerability to early death. If I destroy the life around me, this will tend to make my own life vulnerable. It is as if my brutal habit of mind attracts aggressive situations and aggressive behaviour towards me.

3. The conditioning effect

Karma ripens in a third way through the effect of actions on the physical and social environment. If I act in a particular way towards others such that it causes them to have particular views of me, then at some time in the future these views will cause them to behave towards me in a certain way. For example, acting aggressively towards the outside world causes the outer world to become more aggressive towards me, and this further fuels my own aggression. So there is interdependence between the inner and the outer, the actor and the world.

An example of this kind of karma is the creation of an environment through the act of killing where the necessities for supporting life are scarce. It is said in the sutras that those who kill tend to be reborn in realms where it is difficult to live, because there is very little there to support life. However, whilst this example is of rebirth into a particular environment, karmic effects could also come about within this very life rather than over the course of lifetimes, since karma will mature whenever the conditions are ripe. Karma does not therefore operate through some kind of cosmic judge who is recording our actions in an accounts book and then deciding to manipulate the universe in order to punish or reward us accordingly. Many Western ideas about karma resemble theism or naïve sentimentality more than the Buddhist view. Karma is a natural law, the actual fabric of the universe. It refers to the way that everything in the universe arises from causes and conditions, the process of 'dependent origination'.

4. The fully ripened effect

In very general terms it can also be said that virtuous actions lead to rebirth in the three so-called 'upper realms' and non-virtuous actions lead to rebirth in the three 'lower realms'. These are described in more detail in the last of the Four Thoughts, 'the defects of samsara', but are also very important for the meditation on karma. Rebirth into these states occurs due to the aspect of karma known as 'the fully ripened effect'.

The upper realms are those of the humans, demi-gods and gods. One is reborn into these primarily through virtuous actions such as giving. There one can experience great happiness and contentment, and humans in particular have the opportunity to practise dharma as we have already seen.

The lower realms are the hell, ghost and animal realms. One is reborn into these as a consequence of acts motivated by hatred, desire and ignorance respectively. A single act of that nature does not guarantee birth in the lower realms but it is still a cause of those states. The lower realms are the ultimate consequence of the accumulation of negative actions.

How long does it take karmic tendencies to mature? Since mind itself, being non-physical, cannot be destroyed, it continues to be embodied until liberation. Thus one continues to accumulate karma, so there is no limit to the ripening of deeds. If karmic tendencies do not mature in this life, they will mature in future lives whenever the conditions are appropriate. Karma is the creator of the world and the creator of our destiny.

How should we contemplate karma, having understood its basic principle? We should contemplate firstly non-virtuous actions and their results and secondly virtuous actions and their results. Usually this is done through reflecting on the ten virtuous and ten non-virtuous actions. However, as before these are primarily pointers rather than exhaustive lists.

The Ten Non-virtuous Actions

Actions are what we do through our body and speech and what arises from mind itself. What really characterises an action as virtuous or non-virtuous is the underlying intention. If the intention is hurtful and abusive of others or oneself then it is a non-virtuous action.

1. To take the life of a sentient being

To kill is a non-virtuous act whether the victim is newly conceived or old, human or animal. Why is this non-virtuous? As it says in the sutras, 'everybody cherishes their own life'. To contrive the death of another, whether directly or indirectly (i.e. by doing it oneself or getting someone else to do it) is to cause suffering. It is important to notice that this is not the same as the reasons given for not taking life in theistic philosophies. For theists, the primary reason why life must not be taken is that God has given it. This does not apply in dharma, because there is no God. So whilst the moral action might appear similar, the underlying view is very different.

There are different levels to the value of life. An ordinary person's life is inferior to that of a buddha's, because a buddha brings more benefit to a greater number of sentient beings. Therefore it would be more sinful to kill a buddha than to kill an ordinary person. Similarly, a human being is more important than an animal. Ultimately, all lives are equal in that all beings have buddha nature, but just as there is a relative gradation between a human and a buddha, so there is between a human and an animal. It is for this reason that in the vinaya, the monastic discipline, a monk or nun who takes human life is immediately expelled from the order. However, if they take an animal's life, then although that is a grave sin, they can purify that sin without expulsion from the order.

Killing might be done out of hatred, desire or ignorance. One might want to wear the skin of a particular animal and so take its life for that reason. It could also be done out of ignorance, thinking that offering up the lives of sentient beings to gods will please them. Again, this points to the complexity of judging the fruit of an action. Even with killing, the fruit will be determined by the underlying motivation, hatred bearing the most serious consequences and ignorance bearing the least.

2. Taking what is not given

This means to steal from others, whether by force or by trickery, or to appropriate that which does not belong to anybody for oneself. Stealing may seem to be done mainly through desire but it could also be done out of hatred or ignorance.

3. Sexual misconduct

This means to sleep with another's partner, to coerce someone into sex, to sleep with a child and so forth. If we examine these actions, we can see that some are graver than others, some are more abusive of other people, and such differences must be understood because different actions will have different fruits. Such acts are grouped together merely for convenience, so that we can examine their nature and realise why we should turn away from them.

These first three comprise the non-virtuous actions of the body.

4. Lying

It seems easy for us to take seriously physical actions, but we are more reluctant to consider vocal actions as having karmic power. However, through language we can change the world, change other beings' minds and even poison the environment. Therefore, speech yields good and bad fruits through the process of karma.

Lying is generally done through the motivation of deceiving others for one's own advantage. It renders others abused and powerless.

5. Slander

Slander is done to damage the standing of another.

6. Harsh speech

This is done to crush somebody.

7. Frivolous speech

This is done to create distraction, to obscure what is important for oneself and others. One might consider that frivolous speech could not possibly have a karmic quality, since it seems to bear no actual harm. However, it is harmful, because the more one indulges in it the more the truth is obscured and it is the truth which liberates. Frivolous speech is usually described in the sutras in such a way as to render much of our normal conversation impossible. Compulsive talk about such things as violence, money and sex are all examples of frivolous speech. Also, the reciting of non-Buddhist rituals is considered frivolous speech from a dharma point of view, but for someone who is non-Buddhist that is not the case if their intention is virtuous.

These four comprise the non-virtuous actions of speech. By examining our motivations for using such forms of speech, we will see how they are non-virtuous and abusive of others, and in the case of frivolous speech, abusive of ourselves as well.

The three non-virtues of mind are covetousness, malevolence and perverse views. These are the roots of all karmic actions which, even if not translated into actions of body or speech, still ripen like any other karma.

8. Covetousness

Covetousness means to wish for something that belongs to somebody else. It is primarily an expression of desire. When it arises, it generates in oneself a perpetual feeling of dissatisfaction and resentfulness of others. If acted upon it becomes the negative actions of body and speech, such as taking what is not given or sexual misconduct, or even taking the life of a sentient being.

9. Malevolence

This means to wish ill upon others. It is an expression of hatred. If acted upon, it could translate into taking the life of a sentient being, stealing from them or hurting them by slander and so on. We can easily see the non-virtuous nature of covetousness and malevolence.

10. Wrong Views

One might not think of wrong views as karmically culpable, but it becomes clear how this is so when one understands what it actually means. Wrong views are described as primarily the denial of the connection between cause and effect. It is also, for those who have heard of and thought about them, a denial of the qualities of the Three Jewels. However, since most of the world has not heard of the Three Jewels this does not usually apply.

How can the denial of cause and effect be morally culpable? We often choose to ignore the connection between our actions and their effects and the way one's actions will impact upon others. However, just because we have become habituated to doing this does not mean it is less culpable. If one understands this then one will always behave appropriately towards others. Otherwise, if one continues not to see the connection between cause and effect, then one will continue to indulge in all ten non-virtuous actions.

The Ten Virtuous Actions

The ten virtuous actions may be simply described as the abandoning of non-virtuous actions. Therefore the first virtuous action is to abandon taking life. However, one could also say it is actually doing the opposite of the non-virtuous actions, which means cherishing and saving the life of other beings, and so on for the rest of the ten actions. Just as negative actions produce all the sufferings of the world, so all the joyful experiences one encounters in the six realms originate in one's virtuous deeds. Since this is so, one should delight in such actions. One realises that happiness is within one's own control. It is possible to attain happiness because I, together with everyone else, create this world from moment to moment. So I should seize the opportunity to do virtuous things which are helpful and supportive of others because all happiness grows from this. As Shantideva says,

> Whatever happiness there is in
>   this world
> All comes from wanting others to
>   be happy.
> Whatever suffering there is in
>   this world
> All comes from wanting one's own
>   happiness.

Reflecting on karma endows us with an understanding of the importance of moral behaviour. As Nagarjuna says in his *Letter to a Friend*,

> Morality is said to be the
>   foundation of all virtues,
> Just as the earth is the support of
>   both the motile and immotile.

If one wants the high spiritual qualities like meditation and wisdom, one must have a moral basis. This does not mean blindly following the rules of a cosmic dictator in the hope of reward, but using one's life creatively to help others. That constitutes moral action in dharma.

Meditation on Karma

To really instill within ourselves a wish to turn away from the ten negative actions and take up the ten positive actions, we should question which of our actions fall into these categories, and reflect upon the results that come from them. The ten non-virtuous actions mature as sufferings in the four ways that karma ripens as previously explained. For example, if one considers killing, one will see how it leads to a tendency to kill, the vulnerability of one's own life, one's environment becoming violent and dangerous, and ultimately rebirth in the hell realms. Reflecting on the ten positive and ten negative actions again and again, one will naturally turn away from harmful actions and act more and more positively.

The Defects of Samsara

THE CROWNING REFLECTION of the Four Thoughts is the meditation on the defects of samsara, in which we begin to understand that the only aim of this precious human life is liberation. We cannot be satisfied with anything less than that, because anything else is part of the unending cycle of frustration and suffering. 'Samsara' means cyclic existence, the repeatedly passing through experiences of frustration and suffering. In the sutras and shastras, this meditation is broken down into three parts, firstly to make it easier for us to consider and secondly because we can distinguish three particular modes in which the defects of samsara manifest. These are known as the three kinds of suffering.

1. The Suffering of Suffering

As the great Sakya master Jetsun Drakpa Gyaltsen has explained,

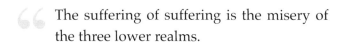 The suffering of suffering is the misery of the three lower realms.

This constitutes the temporary entrapment in the animal, hungry ghost and hell being realms. These three are termed 'lower' realms because they do not have the great potential and freedom of human life. They are temporary because all states in samsara are impermanent. Even if one finds oneself in the realm of hell, at the time it seems that it will endure for an eternity but it is actually impermanent. No situation lasts forever.

Where do these lower realms come from? Their cause lies within our own mind. This is why Shantideva says,

> Did anyone deliberately make
> The weapons of the hell-beings?
> Who made the molten iron
>   ground?
> Where did these hosts of demons
>   come from?
> The Sage has taught that all these
>   things
> Come from a nonvirtuous mind.

1A. Hell

If at the time of death aggression is the dominant imprint in our mental continuum, we will experience rebirth into the hell realms. The traditional description of these in the sutras divides them into eight 'hot' and eight 'cold' hells, four, five or six 'neighbouring' hells and an infinite variety of 'occasional' hells. They are characterised by immense physical and mental suffering.

Jamgon Kongtrul describes the hot hells thus,

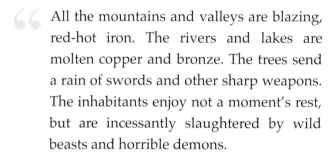

> All the mountains and valleys are blazing, red-hot iron. The rivers and lakes are molten copper and bronze. The trees send a rain of swords and other sharp weapons. The inhabitants enjoy not a moment's rest, but are incessantly slaughtered by wild beasts and horrible demons.

We must understand of course that these depictions are primarily tools for reflection rather than descriptions of some truly existent land. One could say that there are actually just as many different hells as there are different sentient beings, because hell is just the projection of the imprints of aggression onto the screen of one's mind. The more one is aggressive to the world, the more appearances will eventually reflect that. Finally the time comes when one dies and is separated from the physical environment. Then the hallucinations of the entire world as one's enemy will arise due to the hateful state of one's own mind. The eight hot and eight cold hells are symbolic devices to reflect that fact.

The descriptions of the hells derive from the culture

at the time of the Buddha, so one might see them as 'medieval' or 'impossible'. However, we need not imagine that there has been no modernisation in hell. The demons in hell may now be wearing sharp suits and have the very latest instruments of torture! The important principle is that aggression will create its own hallucinations according to one's particular mental and cultural conditioning. One cannot then deny the reality of hell since one carries the seed of it right now in the form of one's own aggression.

1B. Hungry ghost

The hungry ghost realm is structured according to the imprint of greed. The hungry ghosts are beings who are trapped by their obsession with objects that they desired in previous lives. Traditionally they are portrayed as beings with deformed bodies, but, as in hell, these are hallucinatory bodies, like one's body in a dream. Nevertheless, they are so deformed that they can neither acquire nor consume enough food to satisfy themselves. Jamgon Kongtrul says,

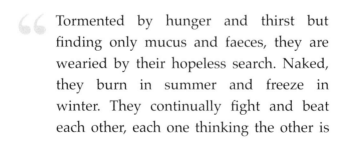

> Tormented by hunger and thirst but finding only mucus and faeces, they are wearied by their hopeless search. Naked, they burn in summer and freeze in winter. They continually fight and beat each other, each one thinking the other is

an enemy. They may live for fifteen thousand human years.

However, the crucial point here is the feeling of being incomplete without something. If obsession is dominant in the mind, one will be reborn as a hungry ghost at the time of death. Due to such obsession in this realm, one experiences a series of hallucinatory episodes of intense deprivation.

1C. Animal

Rebirth in the animal realm comes about through the defilement of ignorance. Specifically, it comes from abandoning the capacity for reflection and choice. Such wilful ignorance corrupts our human status because the chief characteristic of true humanity is the ability to choose. If one loses that, one will decline to a form of embodied life that lacks such freedom, i.e. animal. From the scientific explanation of biological evolution we can see that there is a physical continuum between humans and animals. If one understands that there is also a continuum of consciousness between all beings, it is not difficult to see how there can be movement between human and animal states.

The suffering of this realm corresponds to its basic defilement, ignorance. As is sadly evident, animals endure life in which they are continually preyed upon. Likewise, they prey upon their fellows, helplessly dominated by instinct. They are often subject to exploitation at the hands of humans because in most cases, animals are not capable of thinking creatively enough to find a way out of these situations. It is true that there is variation in the degree of suffering of different animals, just as there is in any of the six realms, yet one can still say that in general animals suffer in the ways just described.

By discussing the lower realms in this way, we can see how each of these realms is carried around with us right now in our hatred, desire and ignorance. We should reflect on them in two ways. Firstly, how can I be sure that if I were to die now, I would not go to these realms? It is easy to see how I could be born there if I consider that I already partly experience them right now in the fluctuation of my mental states between hatred, desire and ignorance. Secondly, one should think that it would be unbearable to be locked in such a realm, so how is it for those who are already there? Thus there is therefore a two-fold outcome of this reflection; a feeling of conviction that one needs to turn away from any behaviour that brings about these states and a feeling of great compassion for anyone already locked in them. This constitutes the meditation on the suffering of suffering.

However, just as if someone were sick with three diseases, it would not be enough to cure only one of them, so it is with the three types of suffering. It is not enough simply to develop renunciation towards the lower realms. We must see suffering in all its forms if we are to generate renunciation. Thus we consider the other, more subtle, manifestations of suffering.

2. The Suffering of Change

This kind of suffering is disguised so that it appears as happiness. It is displayed in the way that every situation which appears to promise lasting success, happiness, wealth or power inevitably reveals itself as suffering in a new guise. We go from disappointment to disappointment, always thinking, 'next time will be the right time'. Occasionally we feel that we have attained something that will bring lasting happiness, but it eventually turns into suffering. This mode of suffering primarily concerns the three higher realms; the human, demi-god and god realms. In these realms there seems to be happiness, so we should investigate whether this is really the case.

2A. Human

One cannot deny that despite fleeting moments of bliss, one is bound by the 'four great rivers' of birth, old age, sickness and death. These are not just possibilities, but are certain to occur. One should consider the inevitability of each of these four unhappy experiences for all beings in samsara.

One is also afflicted by other forms of suffering, such as the struggle of maintaining the things in my life that I hold dear. Or the fact that I cannot always avoid being separate from those who are close to me, whom I love. Even if I manage to stay with them throughout the course of this life, we will inevitably part at the end of it. Friendships and relationships are said to be like people meeting in the market place during the day. At the end of the day all must separate. Furthermore I cannot avoid associating with those whom I dislike. There is also the discontent of not being able to acquire the many things I strive to attain, such as money, relationships or respect.

If one thinks that the suffering of change is unfair, one should remember that there is no god who is creating such things, it is just the nature of samsara. As Lord Buddha said,

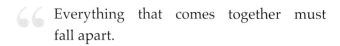 Everything that comes together must fall apart.

The world will not always go according to my wishes and I cannot control events and opt only for the pleasant. The fundamental delusion of ego is that it is in charge, and so it keeps getting frustrated when the world is not in accordance with its designs. In these ways we lock ourselves into this prison cell of samsara.

One reflects upon the suffering of change by looking at one's life, one's motivations and one's experiences and identifying if any aspects of them are free from this description of suffering. How much of my life is given to creating suffering for myself or experiencing it?

2B. Gods

The two other higher realms, the god and demi-god realms, are not physical but mind-made states like the hell and ghost realms. In the sutras, they are described in terms drawn from Indian mythology, so that the god realms are named according to various Vedic gods. This does not imply that we would experience them exactly as described. If dharma had grown up in the West, it would draw upon European mythology. Perhaps in a Christian culture one would think of the god realm as being like the Christian description of heaven. The point of the descriptions is to allow us to develop conviction that experiences of that nature are possible at the time of death if one's mind is saturated by the appropriate causes.

In the god realms, one will experience temporary states of power or bliss. However, since such states are impermanent, like every other state in samsara, they are irredeemably flawed. It is said that samsara is like a burning house, in which every floor is burning with suffering. These reflections allow us to see through the deception of the transient happiness of the higher realms.

The pleasures of the god realm derive from a mixture of virtue and pride. If one practises moral discipline and makes many offerings, one's mental stream will become saturated with virtuous imprints that will come to fruition as long states of bliss, in which one seems completely undisturbed by suffering.

Also, one can produce states of continual bliss through certain types of concentration meditation but have no insight or understanding. This is how one attains rebirth in the god realm through virtue.

The other constituent of the god realm is pride. Having been reborn there, one will feel that one has attained a permanent reward, that one has finally 'made it'. This pride is illustrated in Lord Buddha's description of the god Brahma. When reborn as Brahma, one does not see anyone else in one's universe. Then later, one sees others and a fantastic conceit arises; the thought, 'I created everybody'. In this way, the gods are subject to a very severe mental delusion of pride.

The suffering of the gods is the impermanence of their experience. No matter how long the bliss seems to go on, it will eventually decline because it is produced from causes and conditions. Just as alcoholic intoxication wears off when the alcohol leaves the body, so when the cause of the heavenly bliss wears off, i.e. the previous virtuous actions, the experience of heaven will wear off. This will cause tremendous unhappiness because one thought that one had completely escaped from suffering, only to be plunged right back into it. So although one might think that it would be fine to be in heaven temporarily, it is said that when they die, the suffering of the gods is actually worse than the sufferings of those in hell. What is the point in aiming for such a state?

2C. Demi-god

The demi-gods arise as a result of practising some spiritual discipline with the intention of achieving power rather than bliss. This lust for power is brought about by jealousy of the success of others. The demi-gods, like the gods, must eventually lose their power. But a further suffering is their continual struggle for more power and status, deriving from jealousy. In mythological terms, it is said that the demi-gods fight with the gods. In Christian terms, it is like the struggle between Lucifer and Jehovah. The gods, who are more powerful, always win such struggles, causing great suffering to the demi-god aggressors. If one takes spiritual practice as a means of acquiring power then although one may acquire it, one will never be satisfied and after death one will be reborn as this type of malignant, powerful being. Thus one should not be seduced into gaining the pleasures of the three higher realms, whether as a human or divine being. These environments, however seemingly wondrous, are no refuge from samara but simply further facets of it. As long as one practises dharma with the thought of privileging oneself then one is still within the 'burning house' of samsara.

3. The Suffering of Conditionality

The final type of suffering is one that is totally hidden except to those with deep realisation. This is the suffering of conditionality, the most fundamental of sufferings. It is the mistaken notion that somewhere in one's body and mind, there exists a self. Lord Buddha said that we could consider a being to consist of a continuous stream of five aggregates or 'skandhas'. These are form, feelings, perceptions, karmic formations and consciousness. The five skandhas are arising and passing away from moment to moment. Ignorance, the root of samsara, is essentially the mistaken attribution of a self to these five continually changing bubbles of body and mind.

To express it in philosophical terms, we imagine that somewhere within these five skandhas, whether in one or all of them, or in some way connected with them, there is an autonomous, permanent and independent self. 'Permanent' means eternal and unchanging. 'Autonomous' means self-controlling and creating its own experience. 'Independent' means not relying upon or determined by any factor external to itself. None of the five skandhas are such and so it is a delusion to believe they could constitute a self. All beings except buddhas have this delusion, regardless of whether they actually articulate it. For example, an animal does not have the ability to say whether or not it believes a self exists in this way, yet it continuously holds such a delusion. This delusion is the root of all suffering because it acts like a magnet, attracting to itself all the sufferings of the six realms. By believing I exist as an independent entity, I have split myself off from the rest of the world and I will suffer as a result of that alienation. Ordinary beings do not realise this fabrication of a self is suffering, believing it instead to be happiness. However, since one has created an impossible tension in believing the five aggregates, which are completely non-self, to be a self, then to carry the burden of this illusory 'I' is suffering. Only Aryas ('Noble Ones'), those who possess the eye of insight, see this suffering of conditionality for what it is. It is said,

A single hair cannot be felt on the palm of the hand, but if it enters the eye causes unpleasantness and pain. Fools, who resemble the palm of the hand, do not feel the hair but aryas, who are like the eye, experience it as misery.

Meditation on the Defects of Samsara

As one familiarises oneself with the reality of samsara by reflecting on all these types of suffering, conviction should arise that there is no security or bliss to be found in any of the possible modes of samsaric existence. However, that is not to say there is no happiness at all. As Shantideva says,

> Quite apart from the fact that the
>   future achievement of
>   buddhahood
> Comes from pleasing sentient
>   beings,
> Can I not see that it brings good
>   fortune,
> Reputation and prosperity?

The thought to please others is an expression of abandonment of self since one puts the wishes of others before one's own. It embodies taking responsibility for others' welfare by opening out to them, accepting their needs and wishes. This leads to genuine happiness, but even that is impermanent.

Once one becomes imbued with a sense that there is no true security or bliss to be found in samsara, a longing for liberation will arise. This longing generates an unshakeable commitment to dharma practice, since it is only through such practice that liberation can be won. Lord Buddha himself made the great renunciation at the age of twenty-nine because he encountered the three messengers of sickness, old age and death. Similarly, contemplating the defects of samsara will be the crucial thing that stimulates us to practise.

In general, we are lazy and we do not do things unless we have to, but if we practise dharma casually, then how much will we do? When things become very nice in our life, we will forget about it or it will seem too difficult and we will give it up. But if we consider that being in samsara is like being in a burning house, then we will do something about it. As Nagarjuna says in his *Letter to a Friend*,

> Should head or clothes accidentally
> catch fire,
> Even while trying to extinguish
> them,

> One should strive towards not
>   taking rebirth.
> There is nothing more pressing
>   than that.

We have been invited to look around the burning house of samsara and see what is going on. We then realise that we must escape, and because of this precious human life, we have the opportunity to do so. We can get out of this house, and we are also going to learn as we proceed that we have to take everybody else with us. By contemplating the lower realms, we realise that other beings are trapped in even worse misery than our own. How can one possibly leave them behind? The intention to become a buddha in order to free others from their suffering is called *bodhichitta*. Therefore, even though bodhicitta is usually treated as a higher teaching than the Four Thoughts, it is actually implicit within them.

Meditation on the Four Thoughts

THE BENEFITS of meditating upon each of the Four Thoughts are explained in Gampopa's *Jewel Ornament of Liberation*,

> By contemplating the difficulty of obtaining leisure and opportunity, you will be incited to dharma.
>
> By contemplating death and impermanence, you will be incited to practise virtue.
>
> By contemplating the inevitable cause and effect of actions, you will be incited to abandon non-virtue.
>
> By contemplating the defects of samsara, you will be incited to accomplish liberation.

One can reflect on the Four Thoughts informally, sitting in an armchair or even on the bus. They can also be meditated upon in a formal session. In that case, one settles the mind for a few minutes, using a technique such as counting the twenty-one breaths. One then ceases the technique and begins to reflect on one aspect of the Four Thoughts. For example, one might choose to meditate on the sufferings of the human realm. One recalls those teachings and thinks about them until they really affect one's heart. It is important to question the validity of the teaching, to test whether we really believe it, and compare it with our own experience. Finally, one settles the mind again. If one knows the prayers of taking refuge and dedication of merit, one can recite these at the beginning and end of the meditation session respectively. Of course, as with all dharma practices, one should rely on the advice of a properly qualified teacher.

The reflections on these Four Thoughts are the main meditations of the hinayana, and so in a sense are a preliminary for the main practices of the mahayana and vajrayana. Yet actually they are more important than the main practices since it is only these that make one a genuine dharma practitioner. Studying the profound view of the madhyamaka or doing the tantric rituals of the vajrayana for example will have no meaning unless these Four Thoughts have arisen in one's mind.

As Patrul Rinpoche says,

  Teachings of body and speech, rituals and

yoga are no good unless one's mind has
been turned to dharma. Therefore again
and again contemplate the Four Thoughts.

Even if one has already started to practise
mahayana or vajrayana meditations, one should keep
returning to the Four Thoughts because they will keep
one's dharma alive. It is easy to become blasé and think
that just because one is performing practices, one is
following the path. But inside one might be completely
untouched by dharma. By returning to these Four
Thoughts, one will see one's own situation mirrored in
them and this will keep one's practice completely alive
and effective. One should also ask oneself to what
extent one has realised them.

These teachings are absolutely essential for the
West, as there is a tendency to subvert the dharma
almost as soon as it comes here by changing it into
something more acceptable to Western notions. To do
so is to take out all the medicine of the dharma. If the
Four Thoughts are excised from the dharma, then
whatever practices one does will be a mere show. If
they remain at the forefront of the presentation of
dharma in the West, then dharma will be wholesome,
pure and virtuous and retain its effectiveness in liber-
ating those who practise it.

Appendix: A Brief Guide to Buddhist Masters Referred to

Nagarjuna (1st–2nd centuries CE) was the originator of the supreme Madhyamaka (Middle Way) philosophical system. His ' *Letter to a Friend'* is widely studied since it is a concise and comprehensive summary of the Buddhist teachings.

Vasubandhu (3rd–4th centuries CE) was originally a follower of the hinayana who converted to the mahayana under the influence of his brother, the great philosopher Asanga. His most famous work is the compendium of dharma, the *Abidharmakosha*.

Shantideva (6th–7th centuries CE) was an Indian monk whose most famous work, *Bodhisattvacharyavatara* (*Entering the Bodhisattva Conduct*) is one of the most influential and esteemed texts of Mahayana Buddhism.

Gampopa (1079–1173 CE) formed the Dakpo Kagyu tradition of Tibetan Buddhism, having accomplished enlightenment through the teachings of his master, the great ascetic Milarepa.

Jetsun Drakpa Gyaltsen (1147–1216 CE) was the third of the five great founders of the Sakya tradition of Tibetan Buddhism. He was a celebrated scholar, saint and yogin who meditated continually and possessed the outer and inner signs of realisation.

Thokme Zangpo (1245–1369 CE) was a monk of the Kadam and Sakya traditions of Tibetan Buddhism. He spent thirty years in retreat around the mountains of Tibet.

Patrul Rinpoche (1808–1887 CE) was the author of the great commentary on the ngondro, *The Words of my Perfect Teacher*. He was also a key proponent of the *Rime* (ecumenical) movement, and his teachings on the Four Thoughts and Bodhicitta are especially prized.

Jamgon Kongtrul (1813–1899 CE) was an exceptional scholar and a highly realised master who was one of the principal founders of the *Rime* movement to which he contributed his *Five Treasures,* containing teachings from all the major and minor lineages of Buddhism in Tibet.

Made in the USA
Thornton, CO
08/28/23 19:37:30